Simple
Pleasures
for

TEENS

DIMENSIONS
FOR LIVING

NASHVILLE

Simple Pleasures for Teens

Copyright © 1997 by Dimensions for Living

This book is printed on recycled, acid-free, elemental-
chlorine–free paper.

ISBN 0-687-11139-0

CIP data available from the Library of Congress.

Scripture quotations noted KJV are from the King James Version of
the Bible.

Those noted NIV are taken from the Holy Bible: New International
Version. Copyright © 1973, 1978, 1984 by the International Bible
Society. Used by permission of Zondervan Bible Publishers.

Those noted NRSV are from the New Revised Standard Bible,
copyright © 1989 by the Division of Christian Education of the
National Council of the Churches of Christ in the United States of
America, and are used by permission.

96 97 98 99 00 01 02 03 04 05 06 — 10 9 8 7 6 5 4 3 2 1

MANUFACTURED IN THE UNITED STATES OF AMERICA

You show me the path of life.
In your presence there is
fullness of joy;
in your right hand
are pleasures forevermore.

—Psalm 16:11 NRSV

One

Organize a group of friends to pick up trash along a lake shore or river.

The Lord reigns, let the earth be glad;
let the distant shores rejoice.

—Psalm 97:1 NIV

Two

$\mathscr{B}$ecome a guardian angel to a younger child in your neighborhood. Send cards, phone, and, most of all, listen.

Let the little children come to me, and do not hinder them, for the kingdom of heaven belongs to such as these.

—Matthew 19:14 NIV

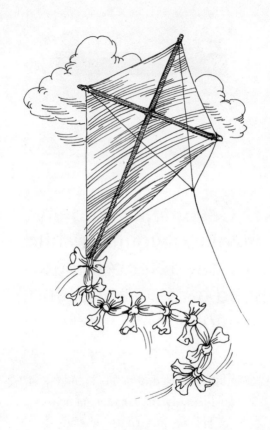

Three

𝓜ake and fly a kite.
You can find a book on
making kites at your local
library.

They shall mount up with wings as eagles.

—Isaiah 40:31 KJV

Four

Interview your grand-parents on audio or video tape. Share the tape with your family on a holiday.

*Grandchildren are the crown of
the aged,
and the glory of children is
their parents.*

—Proverbs 17:6 NRSV

Five

$\mathscr{O}$ffer to walk the dog for a neighbor who is ill.

Let all your things be done with charity.

—1 Corinthians 16:14 KJV

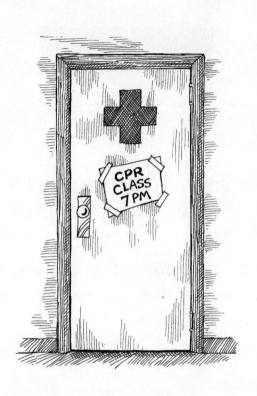

Six

*T*ake a CPR course at your local Y or Red Cross center.

Whenever we have an opportunity, let us work for the good of all.

—Galatians 6:10 NRSV

Seven

*H*ave a movie marathon. Ask friends to rent videotapes around a theme (seafaring, the old West, musicals). Provide soft drinks and popcorn.

Don't let anyone look down on you because you are young, but set an example for the believers in speech, in life, in love, in faith and purity.

—1 Timothy 4:12 NIV

Eight

*V*olunteer in the church nursery.

We continually remember before our God and Father your work produced by faith, your labor prompted by love, and your endurance inspired by hope in our Lord Jesus Christ.

—1 Thessalonians 1:3 NIV

Nine

*A*sk an older neighbor to teach you a skill.

Make it your ambition to lead a quiet life, to mind your own business and to work with your hands . . . so that you will not be dependent on anybody.

—1 Thessalonians 4:11-12 NIV

Ten

$\mathscr{P}$lan a "Cousins" Day. Invite all your cousins to spend the day. Play games, watch movies, make pizzas and cookies.

It shall be a jubilee for you: you shall return, every one of you, . . . to your family.

—Leviticus 25:10 NRSV

Eleven

Cook a simple dinner for the adult(s) in your house. Serve it by candlelight.

Honor your father and your mother.

—Deuteronomy 5:16 NIV

Twelve

When you visit a fast food restaurant, buy the children's meal. Start a collection of the toys included.

Be *joyful always*.

—1 Thessalonians 5:16 NIV

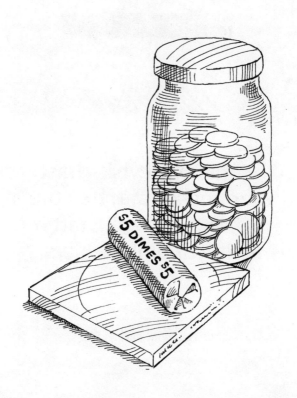

Thirteen

*S*ave all the dimes in
your pocket change until
you have enough to buy a
favorite compact disc.

*As he . . . drew nigh to the house, he heard
music and dancing.*

—Luke 15:25 KJV

Fourteen

Clean out your closet (and the rest of your room). Give your discards to charity or have a yard sale.

Share with God's people who are in need.
Practice hospitality.

—Romans 12:13 NIV

Fifteen

*J*oin a walk, run, or bike ride for charity.

I can do everything through him who gives me strength.

—Philippians 4:13 NIV

Sixteen

Go through your family's snapshots. Make a photographic story of your life.

The boundary lines have fallen for me in pleasant places; I have a goodly heritage.

—Psalm 16:6 NRSV

*S*eventeen

*R*esearch and observe obscure National days; for example, National Yo-Yo Day, National Ice-cream Day, Donald Duck's birthday.

Commemorate this day.

—Exodus 13:3 NIV

Eighteen

Wash the family car.

You received without payment; give without
payment.

—Matthew 10:8 NRSV

Nineteen

Take a "coin walk." Start from your front door; flip a coin at each intersection. Heads means a right turn, tails a left.

Along unfamiliar paths I will guide them.

—Isaiah 42:16 NIV

Twenty

*R*ent skates and learn
to roller blade.

And the streets of the city shall be full of boys
and girls playing.

—Zechariah 8:5 KJV

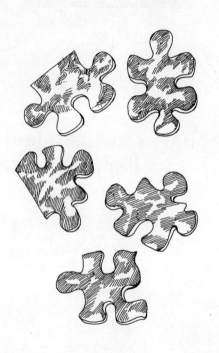

Twenty-one

Work the hardest jigsaw puzzle you can find. Pass it along to a neighborhood center when you have finished.

Endurance produces character, and character produces hope, and hope does not disappoint us.

—Romans 5:3 NRSV

Twenty-two

Train your dog to catch a Frisbee.

*Whoever is joined with all the living has hope,
for a living dog is better than a dead lion.*

—Ecclesiastes 9:4 NRSV

Twenty-three

$\mathscr{E}$very time you go by a craft store, pick up their free patterns and instructions. Accumulate these in a pretty binder for a friend who enjoys crafts.

There are "friends" who pretend to be friends, but there is a friend who sticks closer than a brother.

—Proverbs 18:24 TLB

Twenty-four

*M*ake up silly riddles.
(How do you spell
Mississippi with only
one *i*? Cover one of
your eyes!)

Then was our mouth filled with laughter, and
our tongue with singing.

—Psalm 126:2 KJV

Twenty-five

*H*ave a family or neighborhood game of hide-and-seek on the night of a full moon.

I will turn the darkness into light before them and make the rough places smooth.

—Isaiah 42:16 NIV

Twenty-six

Write a letter to your kindergarten teacher.

Do not let loyalty and faithfulness forsake you; bind them around your neck, write them on the tablet of your heart.

—Proverbs 3:3 NRSV

Twenty-seven

Start keeping a journal,
even if you only record
the weather each day.

*My mouth shall speak of wisdom; and the
meditation of my heart shall be of
understanding.*

—Psalm 49:3 KJV

Twenty-eight

Go to used-book stores.
Buy for yourself and find
great inexpensive gifts.

Of making many books there is no end.

—Ecclesiastes 12:12 KJV

Twenty-nine

$\mathcal{S}$it with your parents in church at least once a month.

Follow the way of love.

—1 Corinthians 14:1 NIV

Thirty

$\mathscr{L}$earn to cook one thing really well.

Prepare for me savory food, such as I like, and bring it to me to eat.

—Genesis 27:4 NRSV